By John Hall Wheelock

POETRY
Dear Men and Women: New Poems
The Gardener and Other Poems
Poems Old and New
Poems, 1911–1936
The Bright Doom
The Black Panther
Dust and Light
Love and Liberation
The Belovèd Adventure
The Human Fantasy
Verses by Two Undergraduates
    (WITH VAN WYCK BROOKS)

CRITICISM
What Is Poetry?

SELECTED AND EDITED BY
WITH INTRODUCTION
Poets of Today VIII
Poets of Today VII
Poets of Today VI
Poets of Today V
Poets of Today IV
Poets of Today III
Poets of Today II
Poets of Today I
Editor to Author: *The Letters of*
    Maxwell E. Perkins
The Face of a Nation: *Poetical Passages*
    from the Writings of Thomas Wolfe

IN PREPARATION
The Past Has Become Paradise (*reminiscences*)

Dear Men and Women

new poems

Dear Men and Women

new poems

JOHN HALL WHEELOCK

Charles Scribner's Sons   New York

PS
3 545
.H33
D4

Some of the poems here included were first published in the following periodicals: *Encounter, Harper's Bazaar, The Lyric, The New Yorker, Poetry: A Magazine of Verse, The Sewanee Review, The Southern Review, The Times Literary Supplement* (London), *Voices*.

The following poems included in this volume appeared originally in *The New Yorker*: "Dear Men and Women" (1963), "Eight Sonnets" (except for "The Letter") under the title "Seven Sonnets" (1964), "The Bathing Beach" (1965), "Amagansett Beach Revisited" in abbreviated form and "Random Reflections on a Summer Evening" slightly abbreviated (1966). Copyright © 1963, 1964, 1965, 1966 The New Yorker Magazine, Inc.

"The House in Bonac Revisited" was first published under the title, "That Fleet Foot."

Printed in the United States of America
Library of Congress Catalog Card Number 66-20460

". . . . . . . *Land der Jugend,*
Land erster Liebe, auch des Todes, wer weiss,
Zu dem immer ich kehr . . . ."

GEORG VON DER VRING

". . . . . *Sauve-toi!*
Pars! Cherche ailleurs! Ce pays n'est pas ton
attache durable!"

JEAN-PAUL DE DADELSEN

To My Dear Friend
Shih-Hsiang Chen
Scholar and Man of Letters

AUTHOR'S NOTE

The poems included in this volume are new and have not previously appeared in book form except for the following four poems: "The Divine Fantasy," now revised, appeared originally in *The Black Panther*; "Storm-Wind," now revised, appeared originally in *The Bright Doom*; "The Letter," and "The House in Bonac Revisited," both now revised, appeared originally in *Poems, 1911–1936*, the latter under the title "That Fleet Foot."

CONTENTS

PART ONE · EIGHT SONNETS

A Garden and a Face	19
So Dark, So True	20
Slow Summer Twilight	21
The Sea's Voice	22
Cloud-Shapes	23
The Letter	24
Bread and Wine	25
In This Green Nook	26

PART TWO

Random Reflections on a Summer Evening	29
A Sun, Which Is a Star	37
The Poet	38
Reflected Light	40
Cat and Mouse	41
Question and Answer	42
Secret Intimations	44
Auscultation	45

The Bathing Beach   46
In the Still of Night   48
The Prayer of the Cricket   49

PART THREE

The House in Bonac Revisited   53
The Divine Fantasy   54
Storm-Wind   63
The Panther   64
The Complaint of an Unappreciated Talent   65
Dismal Observations   66
The Plumber as the Missing Letter   67

PART FOUR

Song   75
The Part Called Age   76
Earth, Take Me Back   82
Amagansett Beach Revisited   83
Telos   87
Dear Men and Women   88
Farewell to the House in Bonac   91
Helios   92

Dear Men and Women

new poems

Part One

EIGHT SONNETS

I

A GARDEN AND A FACE

The countryside that I love best is here,
And in this countryside a certain place,
And in this place a garden and a face
That in the garden sometimes will appear—
It is the gay face of the gardener, dear
Beyond all others; she it is will brace
The drooping vine-branch, grant the weeds no grace,
In the full green and glory of the year.

Great trees encircle her; her praise shall be
The thrush's song; the sea-wind for delight
Buffets her cheek while, massive in its might,
Around these island solitudes the sea,
Chanting, like voices from eternity,
Will shake the shore with thunders, day and night.

I I

SO DARK, SO TRUE

You turn to me with the old childlike, shy,
Questioning glance that first, in boyhood, took
My heart in bondage to those eyes—their look,
So dark, so true, be with me till I die!
From meadowy land, the meadow-lark's clear cry
Brings back, like something in an old story-book,
The days of our lost youth, and hours that shook
Their dear delight upon us in passing by.

Though these are ended, though life, that stays for none,
Must now flow on in others, shall we demur
That had such bounty of happiness from her,
In years together and hours that made us one!
Blessèd be they in whom life's ardors run—
Great life, whose temporary abode we were.

III

SLOW SUMMER TWILIGHT

Slow summer twilight. Darkening branches loom
Beyond the window. Your belovèd head
Bends over the pale page by lamplight, shed
Like a soft aureole round it in the gloom.
Kind destiny holds back the stroke of doom;
We are together, though no word is said,
We are together, and are comforted—
A peace, stronger than joy, fills all the room.

Outside, the darkness deepens, and I guess
What darker things the years may hold in store—
Watching your face, even lovelier than before
Age had given it this grave tenderness
Love stretches hands toward, that would shield and bless
A face, once young, in age loved all the more.

IV
THE SEA'S VOICE

Our talk has been all banter, to-and-fro
Of raillery, the bland mischief of your smile
Still leads me on, with nonsense we beguile
An empty hour: we speak of So-and-So,
Of Eliot and Michelangelo,
And of James Jones, his high, pedantic style—
And touch, by chance, after a little while,
Upon some sadness suffered years ago.

Now your eyes darken, turning serious,
As thoughts of the long past, by memory stirred,
Waken—life's venture, tragic and absurd,
How strange it is, how brief, how hazardous.
Far-off, the sea's voice says it all for us,
Saying one thing forever, barely heard.

V

CLOUD-SHAPES

What huge phantasmagoria of cloud
And travelling moon works magic in the east!
Now gulfs of night, cloud-shapes of man or beast,
Grow bright or dim, with light or dark endowed
As the moon floods them, riding clear and proud,
Or pales, cloud-prisoned, soon again released—
Toward her they drift, diminished or increased,
Becoming now her nimbus, now her shroud.

Some night—and time will have annulled us then—
These things shall be once more: the moon will shine
Through shifting cloud-rack, casting silver-fine
Luster upon strange shapes of beasts and men—
And we not there to watch, ever again.
Come closer now, and lay your hand in mine.

VI

THE LETTER

The night is measureless, no voice, no cry,
Pierces the dark in which the planet swings—
It is the shadow of earth's bulk that flings
So deep a gloom on the enormous sky;
This timorous dust, this phantom that is I,
Cowers in solitude, while evening brings
A sense of transiency and how all things
Waver like water and are gliding by.

Now, while the stars in heaven like blowing sand
Drift to their darkness, while oblivion
Hushes the fire of some fading sun,
I turn the page again—and there they stand,
Traced by love's fleeting but victorious hand,
The words: "My darling, my belovèd one."

VII

BREAD AND WINE

We breakfast, walled by green, as in a bower;
Across the window-pane cloud-pictures float,
A trumpet-vine hangs there, a ruby throat
Glimmers, and is gone. Wind rocks the shaken flower.
The supper hour here is a golden hour:
Light gilds the treetops, eastward the remote
High clouds shine rosy gold, the oriole's note
Falls goldener, falling from his elm-tree tower

Oh, in this green oasis here, we two
Together still—whatever fate provide,
To be together still! In humble pride,
I break the bread and share the wine with you,
Knowing, even as the disciples knew,
Love's very presence sitting at my side.

VIII

IN THIS GREEN NOOK

In this green nook and cranny hidden away
From time the ever-watchful, we have grown
Wiser in age, clung closer for our own
Defense against the inevitable day
When time shall part us, time that grants no stay
For natural grief's sake, which not we alone
Shall have endured, and questioned the Unknown,
That deigns no answer, question as we may.

The old inexorable mysteries
Transcend our sorrow; no mere discord jars
That music, which no lesser music mars—
It was enough to have made peace with these:
To have kept high hearts among the galaxies,
Love's faith amid this wilderness of stars.

Part Two

RANDOM REFLECTIONS ON A
SUMMER EVENING

All day the bird-song here has seemed
The praise and description of this sunny countryside;
Now, with the coming of the stars—
Revelation of the mournful depths of heaven,
Revelation of the truth—those gay voices
Falter, fall silent; a pensive silence,
Soundless as dew, a vague malaise descends,
Quieting all. No matter. In the early morning,
While yet the weather holds, while yet the planet Venus
Sparkles like a jewel on the breast of dawn,
Let us go walk in the woods: the wind
Stirs the top leaves, they rustle, they murmur together,
They clash, like waves of the sea, are still
As the wind stills—a crow rises, cawing,
And fades out of the copse like an evil thought,
Or a hermit-thrush, very far away,
From some towering oak lets fall
His bell-like music.
How good it is to ramble
Through leaf-green woods, or in autumn
Before the trees turn bald, when the colors
Of autumn still flame on the boughs; in winter too,
Under the tracery of bare branches,
While down the face of the rock
The waterfall hangs mute, and the tender brooks
Wear a new skin of ice—the mountain

[29]

Will mirror your voice there, as a mirror echoes
Your face.
                    How good it is to walk
By the strict sea, by void extension
Pressed to the point of absurdity; such vastness
Is supernatural, you await
Almost the feet of an angel treading the blue
Floor of trampling waves—he is
Your dead child-brother, and comes,
With averted face, not to blind you, and folded wings,
Over the level plain, the huge hollow of heaven
Would serve as his canopy. But, of course,
No miracle occurs; better
The loved, familiar things:
Soft ocean odors, space, light, rustling subsidence,
Whisper and hush of fawning waters
Along the shore that terns
Travel with downward head as if cogitating
Their scribbled hieroglyphs there, cast shells, driftwood,
Detritus, old sea-wreckage—the sandy beach
Flows, lion-colored, evenly on
Between the green of the dunes and the changing
Blue-green of the sea. The sea
Can be tragic when roused, has a longer memory
Than that of the wind; their encounter ended,
The wind will hush and the stars come out, not so easily
The sea forgets—hear then, long after,

The restless cry of waters passion-worn
Pleading for rest.
                    How strange the world is!
In the evening, the moon—whose orbit
Feeds parasitic upon earth's ampler orbit—
The gaunt skull of the moon, peers out
Or hides in hurrying cloud, bats
With their lopsided flight cut figures on the air,
Slipping and sliding like the town drunkard,
Tom Swain, who swears he saw,
At dawn, the clouds playing leapfrog, and got so excited
He lost the way home. Thunder
Growls in the west.
                    Now, in sky-crowding cities,
Under the neon's glare, under
The calcium light's demented moonlight, down
Canyons that cleave and rim
The city's massive rock, the sluggish
Man-swarm moves, the sluggish
Traffic, like impeded blood
In senile arteries, moves. Here man
Has elected to dwell among his engines, here
Man's cleverness is all, he lives
In the shadow of monster shapes,
Created by him, that belittle him.
Strange beauty is here, sinister
Beauty that is man's own—see, from some towering mass,

As from some tower of time, watchful,
Two solemn eyes of light
Look seaward with incorrigible stare,
Questioning heaven.
                    In Kennedy,
The fan-jet rouses, slowly
Trundling its ponderous body, the span of enormous wings,
Rigidly spread, the stiff machine,
Ungainly on the ground as an albatross, rumbles
Toward the runway; wheels,
Manoeuvring for position; vibrates like an angry
Hornet; races the runway; is airborne, climbs,
Enters the palace of pure light,
The soundless shadeless empyrean
Above earth's filth and tumult. Soon
We are over the arctic highlands, wolves
Howl in the forest; in Africa
The elephant trumpets his desolate call, the panther's
Scream tortures the night. Oh, this animal lamentation
Heard round the planet—cries
Wrung out of rage, out of lust, out of hunger—only
The birds make music for joy, only
The insect orchestras draw their bows
Over the thighs of longing, only
The deer, the rabbit, the snake, comprehend
The value of reticence, the fish
The vanity of words: in the cool crystal
Of inland streams, in the dusky

Underworld ocean forests or dark
Quiet of deeper waters, oblivion
Of the hushed sea, they drift in silence
Or devour one another with remarkable rapidity, indifferent
To all sense of decency; in warmer waters
The octopus, a bald upside-down head,
With tentacles writhing like the Medusa's hair,
Hangs motionless, the grinning
Shark turns over to attack.
                    How beautiful
The clouds are: the great thunderheads
Piled, one on the other; the lesser clouds, hastening
Like messengers through heaven; clouds
Kindled by dawn or sunset—abysses of flame, portals
Opening on blue paradise; chiaroscuro
Of darkening cloud; luster
Of cloud around the moon; the upper strata,
Sand-ribbed or scaled like fish; whorls,
Flourishes, shreds of cloud unravelled by wind; high
Peace of exalted cirrus. How strangely
Clouds, at a certain moment, in a certain light, perhaps,
Will rouse us as to remembrance of something lost
That yet was there always, a sense
Of how we are part of things, stars, grass, earth,
And they of us. Oh, to move
Among the clouds and above them, to pass through the universe
As a god might, and taste
The whole of it in its splendor, to discover

New worlds, and new races on them, beings
That have some kinship with us, and so break
Our long solitude here, upon
This lonely planet!
                          Where
Are they that are yet to be? Alicia,
Dear unborn child, your face
Haunts the darkness before birth. What generations
Lurk there, or speak to us
In wind or water, riffle of leaves, what millions
Wait in that dark and silence to which
The dead return! Truly,
Our home is among the unborn, there we find refuge
After this temporal dream. To each,
One taste of it, one life,
One only. No foreknowledge,
No memory after. It shall *not* have been.
The moment here is all.
                                How strange a thing time is,
Forever going and coming: the prow of the ship
And the stern of the ship move in separate waters
Yet are one ship and always
Travel the same water, and we, who live
Outside of time in dreams, live also
In a past and a future that form
The ever-continuing present. Dreamlike, the past is present
In the memories of an old man: the face of the mother
Bending over his cot; the first day at school,

Its pride, its terror; the first
Kiss of solemn first love—the grave eyes
Burning, so near, beyond him; faces of women
From the after-days; faces
Of friends, living or dead; face
Of the darling friend and more than friend, belovèd
Face, by half-light known, glimmer
Of cloudy breast, pale thigh—oh, nevermore
Between the dear body and the stars to confide
Life's sorrowful secret, never
Throughout all time again to share
The incommunicable moment!
                How full of sadness the world is,
How full of evil and horror! At the jungle's edge
The python slowly subdues
The body of the struggling fawn; the spider
Kisses the moth to sleep, and sucks
The life from her paralyzed victim; foul
Diseases dry up the sap
In the blossoming tree, the marrow
In the bones of a child—the lower
Preys on the higher, the bacillus would bring down
A Mozart, no favors are shown,
Catch-as-catch-can is the rule—whirlwinds and earthquakes
Devastate earth; well reasoned
Insanities are abroad; though vampires, succubi,
Lamias and gorgons no longer
Harrow the world, demonic forces

Put on the mask of humanity and, as men,
Instigate wars; man
Becomes the enemy of man, far under
In hidden vaults are ranged
The eggs that shall hatch death, his bombers
Are on the alert, the brute
Fury of violated matter shall be unleashed
Against mankind; our galaxy
Is rushing, almost with the speed of light,
Nowhere; there is, we are told,
No sense in things. But in our woods
There are pheasants, young ones—listen, beyond the thicket,
The tender cluck of the hen pheasant urging them on.

A SUN, WHICH IS A STAR

"A sun, a shadow of a magnitude,"
So Keats has written—yet what, truly, could
Come closer to pure godhead than a sun,
Which is a star! Ours not the only one,
But ours, but nearer, so that we can say
We live by starlight the night takes away,
Leaving us many stars in place of one
Yet with less starlight than there was by day
Before that nearer, brighter, star had gone—
And if those others seem too far away,
Too high to care, remember: All we are,
All that we have, is given us by a star.

THE POET

He is an eye that watches in secret, an ear that would
Listen for what can only be overheard,
A mouth to tell us something we have forgotten—in a word,
To tell us all over again
Something we always knew. Oh, if he only could!

This is his torment and supreme
Challenge: for words are clumsy symbols, inadequate,
And reality is subtle and very great—
Greater by far than we have guessed
Is everyday reality, stranger than any dream.

Deep in him always the intuition is there
That something more than what is seen and heard is meant,
Something lost with the innocent
Delight and wonder that habit will destroy,
And which to recapture is his prime despair.

Slant moonlight on a meadow of cocked hay
Toward dawn, or sunlight falling through still apple trees,
What nudges him here, what speaks from these?
The silence of the stars or of the dead,
What is it trying to say?

The cacaphonic roar
Where Broadway and Forty-second meet,
The sombre flow of bodies through avenue and street—
These are things will bear much thinking about,
They are what they seem and something more.

Oh, to discover the formula, the device,
That will give us back forgotten reality again,
So we may share it with others then—
By the flow of a line, the fall of a word, to re-open a door,
If but for an instant, into lost paradise!

Such is the constant dream that keeps him strong
Through days of labor, sleepless nights,
Strange miseries and delights—
It is the cause of many a wound he takes,
The perpetual hope behind his song.

Living, he may be widely heard and become well known,
Or his fame wait upon days that are yet to be.
Dead, the branch he clung to on life's tree
Will tremble a little, for a little while,
Like a branch from which some bird, a nightingale perhaps, has
    flown.

I have come to the time that has more of the moon than the
    sun—
The road leads on through night,
The time of reflected light,
Recollection of remembered longing and delight.
Oh, but for my darling, my dear,
How truly I were alone:
The faces from which love smiled at me
Are taken, one by one—
Many whom I have loved are gone.
I think of them every day,
Of her who cast crazy life away,
Of him who died with promises still to keep;
And sometimes I think of you
With whom youth died too,
With whom the morning-stars fell asleep.

CAT AND MOUSE

Detestable plan, intolerable cruelty
Of the strong to the weak! Yet so nature disposes.
Unanswerable, the look in the dying eye
Accuses the eternal injustice even as it closes.

QUESTION AND ANSWER

Yes, this is the place, and there is the great oak-tree
I climbed as a boy, on the drear dead branches now
A sinister evening-star stares downward fixedly.
> All shall be taken.

And here is the house: the gardens lie waste and bare;
The nymph of the fountain is fallen; in chamber and hall
No voices, no laughter; no footstep now upon floor, upon stair.
> All shall be taken.

And can *this* be the room where, oh, such eons ago,
A young man grieved and exulted, can *this* have been me?
I need wonder no more what it's like to have died, who now stand
here and know.
> All shall be taken.

How slowly we die, how many a well loved face
Time takes and, in taking, has taken a part of us too!
The stars have grown dimmer, the earth has become a less
friendly place.
> All shall be taken.

Like swallows when summer is over, like the clear light
Of morning that fades into dusk, they vanish away,
And our autumn is on us, a gradual darkening, the first chill of
night.
> All shall be taken.

Has the journey no end? Have I come already so far,
Trudging on, trudging on forever, only for this:
To stand in the country of age, under a fading star?
             All shall be taken.

Do we pass from nothing to nothing? Is the moment between
The only moment we have? Before it, is nothing.
After it, nothing. The moment itself will never have been.
             All shall be taken.

SECRET INTIMATIONS

What has the wind told the boughs that they rock and they sway
As with boisterous laughter? What has it whispered the leaves,
Flustered and flurried as girls half delighted, half shocked,
By some scandalous story?

AUSCULTATION

In the cavern of thy breast,
With alternate ebb and flow
Lifting, lapsing, without rest,
The quick wave goes to and fro.

Where the heart of life sustains
The dear being that thou art,
Where the sovereign rhythm reigns
In the tumult of thy heart,

There I hear, in love and awe,
Bending to thy quiet breath,
How life's sea with sullen roar
Plunges, and pours on toward death.

THE BATHING BEACH

As Aphrodite, the mother of love, from the curled sea-wave
Rose, so this one, bikini-clad, goes down to the sea.
The tender budding of the young breasts held firm by the narrow
    bra,
The hollow of the belly naked, the pale hair
Straight as still rain or over the balanced shoulders blown,
She enters the waters, which to receive so sweet a burden
Cling as they part—the wallowing waters where girls and boys
Shout to each other, battling the breakers, riding
The long chute of the rollers that crumble along the shore.
Beyond, in the farther quieter reaches, the swimmers move
In rhythm with the sea's motion; the slow swell
Of the billow rises like a great breast, like a great breast subsides,
Under a boundless heaven of wandering cloud—no voice,
No sound, is here. But, landward, the tireless combers
Pound and pound, to shatter in surges of foam, sun-glittering
    spray,
Cannonade and shock of plunging waters; the huge
Serpent of the world there folds and unfolds his monstrous coils,
With rustle and drag of interminable masses irresistibly moving,
Shifting position, endlessly shaking the ocean bed,
Drowning the happy shouting of boys and girls, the excited
Shrieks of youngsters rolled in the sea-spume, drowning
Old Triton's horn, perhaps, or the whinny of father Poseidon's
Stallions, there where his chariot, churning the level brine,
Far out, moves swiftly over stilled waters, drowning
The plantive radio music from the near beaches:

The choral blues, their savage and sorrowful celebration
Of love's adorable body, its taunting loveliness,
To the brute desecration and sensual mystery foredoomed—
The chant of the praise of life in act, its cruel necessities,
And the ache of desire. This music, before the oceanic thunder
And smash of the sea, falls silent. Light, light,
Along the horizon; on blue-green waters, on dune and foreland,
Light; and on shoulders that gleam through the surf, on gliding
Wing and drifting sea-cloud; while, over all, Helios, father
And god, from his golden lyre pours heavenly harmonies.
Joy, oh joy of the laughing bathers, joy
Of wind and wave, of sea-bird skimming the wave-crest,
Joy of clash and tumult, clamor of conflicting waters
In massive undulation marching, thud of breakers,
Labor of the sea, shuffle and wash of withdrawing surges,
Salt spume, sea-odor, spindrift, scatter of sea-spray,
Clang and shudder of the sea, rocking the old foundations,
πολυφλοίσ βοιο θαλάσσης, the sea, the sea!

IN THE STILL OF NIGHT

In the still of night when the high stars shone through,
At the cry of a whip-poor-will while the house slept,
At that familiar cry I thought of you
And of how long it was since I had remembered you,
My darling, and I wept.

THE PRAYER OF THE CRICKET

In the darkness I make my music for myself alone,
I sing for the joy of singing.
Father, of whose seed I am,
The fire in my heart is from you.
When you return in glory, at daybreak,
Grant me—by then perhaps grown tired of song—
Peace, benediction of your light.

Part Three

I am in love with the impossible:
From the beginning, I have tried to bring
Into the toils of language the fierce thing
No word may gather and no tongue may tell—
And it was in this room that first the spell
Was cast upon me for a curse, to wring
My heart in labor and in suffering,
Under these rafters that I love so well.

How many a night, how many a lonely year,
With mind grown bitter and with blood gone dry,
I have wrought these cunning toils! Nevertheless,
All longing was repaid, all bitterness,
In moments when my heart stood still to hear,
Even for a moment, that fleet foot go by.

THE DIVINE FANTASY

Brother, from what dim world of lonely light,
Trembling on heaven's pinnacles to-night,
Is lifted your sad face of love while you
Stare upward toward me, staring upward, too,
At that faint flame which is your home, between
The leafy branches of these poplars seen—
So hushed, so far! Perhaps, to-night, you scan
Your starry heaven for the star of Man,
High in the trellis of eternity
And glittering arches hung—perhaps, like me,
You, too, look up and wonder. Is it fair,
That world of yours? Are there great cities there,
Clamorous millions, hearts that beat as these,
Clear meadows and far mountains, shoreless seas,
Shadows of moving armies, thrones that shake?
Does the heart burn for love there, does it break?
Tell me, are there hushed gardens, quiet tombs,
And holy poets weaving at their looms
The old, dim wisdoms that outweary time—
And saints, and hallowed saviours, the sublime
Ardors and fortitudes beyond belief?
—All blotted out by one small poplar leaf
In the light wind of languid summer stirred!
Brother, what news out of the night, what word,
From the frontiers of mind beyond our ken,
Of mysteries unimagined yet of men,
Compassed by travail of your spirit? Oh,

Could you but reach to us, could we but know
Across the imperturbable old Dark
Some answering glimmer of the ancient spark
Lifted, some token, tangible to sense,
Of the indomitable intelligence
Inhabiting matter—language visible,
Crying, "Eternity, and all is well:
Brother, be of good cheer—we, too, have known!
Not lonely moves, not utterly alone,
Your sad fraternity, through the dark of God,
But the confederate legions are abroad;
Life's flag advances on the starry way,
And consciousness, still battling, still at bay,
Holds the bright forts against oblivion—"
What answering thrill would round the planet run!
For we are one—all consciousness is one,
Whatever form it wear, however dressed
In gray or glamour, in whatever breast
It house its longing: glimmering, it moves
Through the green wave; it stamps with startled hooves
The upland pastures of the world; and soars
In heaven, with the eagle; on bright shores
It basks a sunny body; or, in dread,
Lifts from the undergrowth a snaky head,
And darts a flickering tongue; it is most clear
In the lark's throat; beneath the grasses here,
That hide the ant, it turns a tiny eye
Around the darkness; scampers, and is shy,
In the scared rabbit; through the murmuring air
Wheels, with the beetle; and, where heaven is bare,

Southward, with the wild crane, at summer's close,
Hungering, an eternal pilgrim, goes
On quests implacable. And from the eyes
Of the poised panther gleam the cruelties
Of its stern need, that roams the world, and rends
With tooth or talon; in the hawk descends
On the stunned squirrel; in the squirrel moans
As the hawk strikes; darkens the earth with bones
Of its own wreck, and, hungering again,
Knows in its body the old spur; for when
Hunger, the shadow cast by death, draws near,
Life, in its many forms, feels the one fear—
And, in the lion's roar at dusk, is heard
The unassuageable, insistent word
Of urgent Being, clamorous to be:
Warring and warred upon; eternally
Mingling and mixed; inextricably blent,
Victor and vanquished, in one sacrament,
Body with body, of delight and death,
It moves in splendor; lifts the shuddering breath
Of the spent stag; and, in the mind of man,
Rebels against the harsh, the cruel, plan—
Flings its frail web of thought across the path
Of suns in heaven, and in holy wrath,
On blood of murdered brothers nourished, still
Thunders to all the world, *Thou shalt not kill!*
And the worm's death is in the robin's song.

And I have seen it in the gnats that throng
Old shadowy forests, in aerial dance;

Or, in the little measuring-worm, advance,
Inch by slow inch, along the swaying stem
Of some exalted flower; or lift the hem
Of the frail butterfly's embroidered cloak,
In gentle breathings that the sun would stroke
Caressingly, with fingers of his heat;
Or, from the dog, yearn upward, and entreat,
With eyes of adoration or of fear,
The great god, Man—"What message, master dear,
From the dim heights beyond me, where you are?"
In the mare's tremulous whinny, in the far
Lowing of cattle from the upland sward,
Or wail of whip-poor-wills, at twilight, poured
On pools of silence plaintively, or cry
Of the lone wolf beneath the glittering sky
Of soundless winter, I have heard the same
Splendor speak forth and utter the one name
Of Life, the dreadful, the magnificent.

All afternoon the passion of heaven spent
On earth its fiery fury, in blind bright
Lightnings of dread, and laughters of delight,
Down shuddering deeps of shaken thunder, where
The delirious longing loosed its sorrowing hair,
Of wind and shower and overshadowing cloud,
Across the belovèd face, in darkness bowed
Or glimmer of light revealed—and cried aloud,
For anger of utter ecstasy, and shed
The wild love of the rushing rain, that sped
To the rapt heart, consenting, of the dim

And amorous earth, who lifted up to him
Drowsed lips of thirsty flowers—and the cup
Of every flower, for joy, was lifted up,
And drank, and swayed. So, tired out at length,
Flagged the bright pulses, and the ebbing strength,
With muttering of remembered thunders, passed
Down the large shores of evening—till at last
The exhausted heaven of twilight from afar
Shone, washed of all her sorrows, and a star
Brooded above the fading storm, and saw
The winnowed reaches deepening into awe
Of gradual darkness, and the fields that lay
All drenched and wearied out at dusk of day
And the worn end of things, while far away
The receding fury moaned.

                              And now they lie
In the same peace around me, and the sky
Holds up her stars; now in the rain-drenched wood
The tree-toad drinks the rain and finds it good,
And trills for joy—the sliding waters grieve
Quietly—now the bat begins to weave,
With intricate motion, on the cloudy loom
Of glamorous starlight mingled and gray gloom,
His dipping flight among the darkened boughs
And leafy vistas, and the little mouse
Furtively hurries through the lane, his eye
Turned up in terror as the owl goes by:
On softest feathers of silence overhead
Flits the dim shadow of the ancient dread,

Hooded and huge, the cruelty of his beak
Bent on old lustful mysteries. A squeak!
A scuffle! Beating of wings—and in the lane,
Silence! and the old wrong is done again,
That was before Adam—the triumphant heart
And the defeated, each one doomed to his part,
They play it through, the old tragedy, where one
Presence still wars and still is warred upon,
Slays and is slain; while fiercely all around
Shakes the eternal love-song, in shrill sound,
Of grasshopper and cricket; sleepless flow
The immortal tides of longing, to and fro,
On waves of music; endless is the prayer
Of life to the belovèd, everywhere
Lifted in adoration; on dark shores
Beats the insistent passion, that implores
The one dear breast of pity or disdain,
To be reborn, to be reborn again,
Nor perish wholly. The blind earth is thrilled
As with glad rites accomplished, deeds fulfilled,
Marriage and mystic union; all along
Her brimming meadows rings the bridal song
Or chant ecstatic—that great heart of hers
Is touched now the eternal longing stirs
From hill to hollow, and hollow to far hill,
In many voices mingled, or the still
Ecstasy of the firefly that trails,
Among the shadows where the starlight fails,
His body's burning love. Forever flows
The dreadful drama to its stately close

And endless ending, the fierce carnival
Of death and passion, wherein each and all
Mix, and are mingled, slaughter, blend, and pass
Each into other—the high poem that has
No end and no beginning, which the one
Self in all living forms beneath the sun,
And on all worlds around it and above,
Weaves on the strands of hunger, death, and love.

I see it all, I hear it all, and lie
Under my swaying poplars, and the sky
Is fretted with frail leaves. The mortal dream
Is in my heart: I hear the night-hawk's scream
Shatter the startled silences, I hear
The owl's clear tremolo rise over-clear—
The mouse's blood along his veins has made
His love-note lovelier and the night afraid
Of beauty's dreadful secret; and I know
Soft shapes of stealth that in the darkness go,
Of furry lusts and gnawing hungers, small
Twittering things obscene, that flit or crawl
In furtive secrecy, vague mouths, and blurred,
Of the night creature or nocturnal bird,
Ambiguous moth and bat-shape—and the earth,
With all her burrows, nooks and nests of birth
Crowded, and wreck of many a perished might,
By the ebbed waters of life's fierce delight
Washed up on shores of silence, spoiled and spurned
Altars, where once the sacred fire burned,
Forms flowing back into the formlessness—

In a supreme embrace, a long caress,
Mixing their bodies with the mother mould—
And all the heaven of stars, around me rolled,
Whose brooding eyes have stared so many an age
Upon this theatre of lust and rage,
Of death and adoration. And a breeze
Rustles the branches of the poplar-trees.

Dear spark, that shinest in the solitude!
One consciousness, that, in the brotherhood
Of all earth's living creatures, movest on
The shaken ramparts of oblivion—
Whose starry cry, across the darkness hurled,
Makes music in the silence of the world!
Life, whose sole splendor in red slaughter spills
The blood of its own breast; in many wills,
Wars on the one will; and, in rage or dread,
Feeds on itself and, on itself being fed,
Shines forth in song and color; gilds the dress
Of the green-fly; and pours its loveliness
In rapture on the earth; in theatres
Of crowded congregation sits—nor stirs—
Watching itself, itself the spectacle;
And builds the swallow's breast, and shapes the shell
And all these mansions of its thought that are
Between the morning- and the evening-star,
On earth, in heaven, or in the glimmering caves
And grottoes of the world below the waves;
Butchers the ox, and, gladdened by his meat,
In the young mother's downward smile is sweet;

Or, sated of its hunger, walks abroad
In symphonies, and poems, and prayers to God;
Sins, and has conscience and, repenting, sins;
And, in the lowly patient spider, spins
Its fragile web; and in these words of mine
Flings out its groping utterance, line by line,
Across the intangible abyss of thought—
With infinite passion, infinite patience, wrought—
Dread Loveliness, be strong in me, be strong,
To sound your dark confession in my song!

STORM-WIND

You came—and like a stormy wind your love
Blew over the lone waters, and the sea
Of my heart's life was shaken violently,
And all the trembling waves began to move,

And cried their love out to the shore, and cast
Their love upon the shore—but you were gone!
Yet still that restless flood is roaring on,
Where once so brief a storm in fury passed.

And still, from the calm heaven of my mind,
My thought, like a great hawk on lonely wing,
Watches those waters laboring, laboring,
In troubled multitude, broken and blind.

THE PANTHER

(In the Jardin des Plantes, Paris)

*from the German of
Rainer Maria Rilke*

His gaze through the bars forever going by him
Has grown so dulled it takes in nothing else.
To him it seems a thousand bars go by him,
That behind the thousand bars there is nothing else.

The soft tread of those strong and supple paces,
Turning in the smallest circle, round and round,
Is like a dance of strength about a center
In which some mighty will stands stunned and bound.

At times, though, the curtain over the pupil
Will lift. Then an image passes in soundlessly,
Passes through the tense stillness of the limbs—
And, in the heart, ceases to be.

THE COMPLAINT OF AN
UNAPPRECIATED TALENT

Consider all the nonsense that has been written since the begin-
    ning of time,
Pile all the books on top of one another,
Toss in a pair of old socks,
A couple of badly scuffed, rubber-heeled oxfords—
And, finally, for good measure, the old corncob pipe.
What does it all amount to?
Nothing any better than much that is being written today—
Certainly, nothing as complex as the creative writing I have done
    during the past few years.
For the merely good is no better than the worst;
And the best—and this is something I'm always arguing about—
Is usually overlooked, and never fully appreciated.

DISMAL OBSERVATIONS
(A *study in half a dozen types of ambiguity*)

The mourning-dove, that sang all evening
To Arthur Senior Jr. here,
Left, this morning, feeling much better,
And won't be back for another year.

The bird-brained geese that I saw heading
Northward, one chilly November day,
Have made me wonder if wonderful nature
Is really as wonderful as they say.

No one can write as well as you can,
Old Cock-of-the-Walk, and that is true
With one exception, and that exception—
What I mean to say—of course, is you.

THE PLUMBER AS THE
MISSING LETTER

(A frolic—with apologies to Wallace Stevens)

Consider Kant's categorical imperative,
Its exegesis, as metaphor for the flawed
Hand-bowl, the clogged hot-water faucet; consider
The absolute assininity of things,
Their grand idea; consider the evening-star,
Pendentive, but to no purpose, importuned
In vain by the crazed householder; and ponder
New ways for swallowing swords. Shall this bring on
The snub event! The invincible nincompoop,
With pomp and stink of belittered Cadillacs,
Conspicuous by his presence, casual
To the point of utter inanity, shall arrive,
Careless and confident and unconcerned,
And always available—but not to you,
Scrounging and screaming, and by no ruse of yours
Dragged through time's keyhole. Truly, when he arrives
He shall be here, and not before, and, coming
Surely and shiftily, not come at all,
Who was here already, and not here, Grand Seigneur
Of the senile bathtub, Princip and Calvador
Of the dripping water-tap—may fate encourage
His early advent. With him he shall bring
Tools, and a helper: monkey wrenches, spuds,
Flush balls and float balls, locknuts, shaft extenders,
Couplings and plugs, female and male adapters,

Bolt-washers, pig-nosed tank balls, and what else
He deems required: then on the bathroom floor
Take station, invite audience. Here conceive
Station as fictive stance, audience as careful
Inattention to the householder's furtive plea,
Swinkum and swankum, blather of this and that,
Nonsensical in its essence, essentially
Preliminary, as eyes to eyelids are—
Quotha, a waste of time, as who should teach,
Presumptuous, his grandam to apply
Suction to ovoids; q.e.d., time lost,
Time that is irretrievable, time paid for,
Time, the bland lubricant permitting passage
To what were else estopped. The stage being set
For the supreme fiasco, witness now
The evasion of event, its pure objective
Correlative: down the back stairs they go,
He and the helper, and is there a job to do,
Don't do it. As in Ashkan of Yucatan
Once, the Kafkan of Oxil, his emissaries,
To Uxmal, Lord of Ashkan, bearing gifts—
Item, four score toucans; item, twelve flutters
Of verdant parakeets, well plumaged; item,
One thousand nine hundred and ninety cockatoos—
Did, counter to said lordship's protestation
And strong demur, to fetch gifts greater still,
Of more illustrious provenance, depart,
So these, the plumber and his helper, departed
To fetch tools overlooked, but with assurance,
"Will be back shortly." The obese and bawdy sun,

Prime breeder of plump figs and squiffy pears,
Of strawberries and warty squashes, patron
Of frolicsome jollification, savage song,
Had from his zenith to the obsequious west
Now condescended, and still the fictive pair
Proves absentee—quocunque modo, missing,
Away, not here. The householder, returning
From promenade at dusk, makes swift ascent
To the smug bathroom, dismally observes
The dripping faucet, the leaking water-closet,
The remnant tools, and, from extreme frustration
Frenzied, falls to his knee-caps, importuning
In vain the evening-star; then to his study
Repairs, and in great volumes gray with dust,
Journals abdominal or hebdomadal,
Encyclopedias and spick quarterlies,
Annals and annuals, or what you will,
Delves with enormous labor and scant wit,
So to discover or devise new ways
For swallowing swords or sword-fish. This in vain,
Hope is abandoned. Then takes up a book
By Wallace Stevens and, tenderly recollecting
The phrase, "will be back shortly," comes across
A phrase by Wallace Stevens, "the supreme
Fiction." Eureka! Stevens at last is clear,
Uncommonly so. Nota: man may audit
The ocean, superintend the evening-star,
Enforce the law of gravity but not
The promises of plumbers. Thus encouraged
By Wallace Stevens, the householder reads on,

A fop of fancy, a bawd of euphony,
Bandmaster of stewed onions, prince of poppets,
As far as page one-fifty-two, when,
Finding himself somewhat beyond his depth,
The verse more ophidian then Ovidian,
And the heat abominable, he falls asleep.
Of what swank paradiso shall he dream,
Land of swart dames seductive, the cohesive
Feminine, woman the universal glue;
Land of chubbed grapes and peaches, land of prime
Poets, de jure some, some few de facto—
Shall not the pumpkins on the pensive boughs
Hang heavier there than here, the birds employ
A brisker breast-stroke, be more nude than here;
More pleasing to the sense, nimbler than here,
The sea's blue thunder, the curved smell of the sea?
His dream shall be of these, of frogs at sunset,
Moonlight upon bald heads, and something more,
Worthier than these, more plausible; but no,
He dreams of oddites, air-conditioned graves,
Serpents that totter, mice that sing soprano,
Of hangnails and of handsaws and of hawks,
The owl's œsophagus, the curlew's pharynx,
And of the calf that laid the golden goose;
Yet, of his dream, the central theme is always
The bathroom fixtures, always of these he dreams,
Fondly, and of the plumber, the supreme
Fiction, till concentrating, in his dream,
All thought, all passion, upon the supreme fiction
As the imagination of the real

Conceived as a fantasy that is itself,
Snoring, he falls asleep all over again,
As you, no doubt, dear reader, already have done.
And so to bed. Enough of this pizzicato,
Strumming of strings, Stradivarian agitation.
Sir, the next music be cock-adoodle-doo.
Explicit "The Plumber as the Missing Letter."

Part Four

SONG

Far wind, old sea-wind, you
That wake me from my dream,
Your soft airs waft to me
Memories of some sea
That I was moving through
Forever, in my dream.
I wake, yet all things seem
So dream-dark, falsely true—
Dark is the night, the dream
Dark, I was moving through.
Oh, what is false, what true?
Oh, that the soft airs blew
A breath from some far sea
To wake me from this dream.

THE PART CALLED AGE

What was this thing called "growing old"? All his life
He had heard about it, had read about it, had seen
Others grow old. He remembered his father's words:
"Someday, when I am gone and you are older,
Perhaps you will understand." 'Perhaps,' he had thought,
Wondering what really there was to understand
In that so improbable state. Dimly he sensed
That life, like an old legend told over and over,
To each of us throughout the generations
Is told for the first time, to each of us
Told once, once only, its tender passages
Of youth, of love, of joy, and that if you listened
Long enough you would come to the part called "age,"
And after that came death. But never to him,
He would think—to others, but never to him, this incredible
Remote event! In the rush and hurly-burly
Of living, there was scant room for thoughts of death,
Much less of age, so that imperceptibly,
Almost as if in the winking of an eye,
The thing happened: waking from the long turmoil
And trance of youth, suddenly you found it there—
Not knowing what had become of the years between,
You found yourself, as now he found himself,
An agèd man pacing his father's acres,
Remembering how his father had said, "Someday,
When you are older, perhaps you will understand."
Was it not all exactly as foretold

Long since? Had it not happened all over again?
He had come to that passage in the old legend so many
Before him had listened to through the centuries—
But, oh, the difference, for now it was told to him,
And it wasn't believable! The tide of summer
Stood high in the land: the fragrance of honeysuckle,
Toward which the painted-lady and fritillary
Spread sunlit wings, mixed with the darker odors
Of earth and ocean; already an early cricket
Began his tentative tune; the humming-bird
Shook dew down from the flower of the trumpet-vine;
And in the woodland, where oven-bird and chat,
Flicker and wood-dove, thrush and vireo,
And an occasional phoebe, were the voices
Of this sea-drowsy country, the wild azalea
Shone like a flame. These were his father's acres,
For so he still thought of them, though now they were his,
And dear and lovely as they ever had been,
Yes, dearer to him even than when in childhood
He and his brother had climbed the ancient oak,
Now fallen, that stood near the house, or when as a boy
He watched, at twilight, from some western window,
The young moon setting behind the sycamore,
While the evening-star brightened and the first bats
Circled the garden—yes, lovelier, dearer now
Almost to the point of heartbreak, for now the heart
Such memories haunted was stricken at every turn.
Things were no longer merely themselves, but all
Echoed one another in endless reverberations,
The past lived on in the present, something unearthly

Had entered the earth, and the swollen springs of feeling,
Long pent in the breast, were straining at overflow.
Now the thrush's song, heard in some earlier summer
With one well loved no longer here, could twist
The heart with an agony keener than any joy;
The familiar sound of the sea, forever shifting
Its weight of waters on far shores, awaken
Memories of that sound, heard long ago
In happier hours. He had come to that part of the legend
Time tells us if we live long enough to reach it,
And it is grave, for in that part of the legend
Those loved and no longer with us will outnumber
Those loved and with us still. He turned abruptly,
Retracing his steps along the path he had come,
Through woodlands of green light and gloom where the small
Wind-flowers flanked the way and, as he went,
Pondered his thoughts. Was it possible this stranger,
This agèd man pacing these wooded lawns,
These well loved acres, was it possible this was he,
The youth who used to walk them? And by what devious
And hardly remembered passages of the past
Had he arrived here? He tried to call up that past,
Go back over those passages in the old legend
That Time was telling him, and rediscover
The way by which he had come. Vague memories
Welled up in him; old episodes, old scenes
From other days long vanished, came back to him;
Faces and forms of the belovèd dead
Appeared before him; like magic-lantern pictures
Cast on the screen of memory, they came

In marvellous procession: Harriet trimming
The Christmas tree; Ned, in their rooms at college,
Bent over some endless book; Sara's shy glance,
On parting; his father laughing at him; his mother
Listening to the new poem. How strange, how dim,
These images were! With all the strength he had,
With all his imagination, he strove to summon
Forth from these images the reality,
To bring before him again, in all their truth,
The darling men and women whose breathing presence
Still vibrated in the heart. But they remained
Beyond his summoning; these, who once had been
So near, so dear, had now become mere figures
In some old legend he had heard about—
And he believed in them as you believed
In the figures in an old legend. Oh, all those words,
Those cries, that life, that love, reaching out to us,
What did it mean, he thought, this show, this pageant
Paraded before the spirit! Was it not all
A monstrous allegory, whose forms and fictions
Were but the symbols of some secret thing
That Time was trying to tell us—we who, ourselves,
Were characters in the story? By now he had come
To the marble bench facing the lower garden,
And he rested there, sunk in his meditations.
The soliloquy of the sea, heard far away—
Sound without end; the excited, rain-sweet, fresh
Chatter of summer birds; slow pace and dazzle
Of summer clouds; the scent of flower and grass;
And the soft breath of summer on his cheek,

Mixed with his thoughts: the inner world and the outer
Interpenetrated and mingled; past and present,
As in the confusion of a waking dream,
Were blent in the one phantasmagoria,
Heightening each other; and more and more they came
Crowding, those echoes and images out of the years—
Faces, faces, of the living and the dead,
Laughing or grave, some tender, some grimacing
As if in mockery—endlessly they came,
A flood of memories stretching the taut spirit,
Too well aware how all would be soon withdrawn,
And straining to hold all. The long, sunlit hours
Found him still lost in reverie. Toward evening,
Like one awakened from a deep dream, he rose
And, leaving the garden by way of another path,
Mounted the slight incline to the old house.
The house he had once compared to "a great ship foundered
At the bottom of green sea-water" now seemed to him,
As it lay there lonely in the sad evening light,
More like a ship on some vast voyage bound
Into the unknown seas of space and time—
He thought of it as a vessel whose prow was plowing
The dark ocean of the stars, the immeasurable, shoreless
Waters of the future. What did that future hold,
He wondered now, for himself and for the world,
In the days ahead? Where was the old ship steering,
Through a darkness such as had never before been known
In the long history of man? There was no foretelling.
There was none could say. But of one thing he was sure:
The fragile network of love that binds together

Spirit and spirit, over the whole earth,
Love—that by the very nature of things
Is doomed, is destined to heartbreak, mortal love,
Which is a form of suffering—here and now,
In its brief moment, yes even in its defeat,
Triumphs over the very nature of things,
And is the only answer, the only atonement,
Redeeming all. Far over, a waking star
Glimmered in the west of heaven. He opened the door,
And entered the house, the ship, where so many others
Had embarked as passengers, where one passenger now,
The dearest of all, awaited him. Quietly
He turned the key in the lock, and gave the good ship
To night and darkness and the oncoming stars.

EARTH, TAKE ME BACK

I have been dying a long time
In this cool valley-land, this green bowl ringed by hills—
The cup of a giant flower whose petals are
These forests round about, still wet
From the fresh April rains.
Night draws on. It is growing dark.
The trees are silent. The hills are dark and silent.
All things fall silent, or look the other way,
When you are dying.
There is a delicate haze over everything.
Soft clouds are floating like water-lily pads
On the dark pool of the sky. Between them
Stars come out . . .

AMAGANSETT BEACH REVISITED

Once more I move among you, dear familiar places,
Pale shores, pale dunes, long burdened by my long love of you—
The sun strikes the great glass of ocean a glancing blow,
The waves are kneeling in the sun-dazzled spaces.
June is upon us: earth and sea
Are brimmed with tidal life; the mackerel now
Throng the Atlantic shallows; from some bough
Inland, the red-winged blackbird sounds his "fleur-de-lis"—
Life, that lifts up
In the green woodland the day-lily's cup,
Wakes in my heart once more,
Imagination spreads wide wings in me.
The blue road of the sea,
The void sea-road that runs
From here to the horizon, now—as once
In earlier summers when I strode along,
Measuring to the sea's rhythm the rhythms of my song—
Beckons imagination on.
In labor and ecstasy,
Beside these waters my best hours were passed:
Walking, I shaped my poem, while overhead
The gliding wing of gull and tern would cast
Wing-shadows, gliding shadows, on the beach;
And it was here that first,
To the night sea's dark monotone,
The lips of love were laid against my own,
Rousing in a boy's heart that ancient thirst,

Unslaked till life is done.
What loved companions, long since gone,
Have walked these ways with me by dune and shore,
What friends who come no more
Have come with me these sandy ways—
Dear men and women of the departed days,
Life's pride and glory, and among them none
Dearer and more loved than one,
Humble in greatness, who walked with me here,
How many a summer, many a year!
His going took some warmth out of the sun.

Where are you, comrades of my youth,
You earlier, you familiar faces,
That do not come again!
The days I live in look for you in vain—
You would not stay to share these days with me,
Or bear him company
Whom time has carven to this mask uncouth.
O cruel and beautiful, O unchanging sea,
All passes, you alone remain:
How bitter is the truth,
How bitter our mortality.

Yet, ah, you blest beaches, blest shores where I have known
Such visitations, such glad comradeship,
Such hours of secret, lone
Sombre communion
With this bleak coast, these wastes and waves of mine,
Of which I am a part, as they of me—

The brute, divine
Unchanging, ever-changing sea—
Was it not worth it to be born,
To have felt this sun, to have drawn this breath!
Is life not worth the price of death!
Death, which we share with the forgotten dead,
With all the billions who have suffered it,
Shall we not suffer it—
In love and dread,
Lie down, make way,
For the unborn, those nameless others yet to be,
More multitudinous than the stars of heaven
And, like them, hidden in our day,
Till, in our night, they shall come forth
In their young glory, and we—
By grace of death's dark stratagem,
This self denied,
The knot of self untied,
All selfhood set aside—
We shall be *them!*

All afternoon, I have pressed
Eastward, toward Amagansett. In the west,
The sun grazes the rim. Two sandpipers
Companion me now along the way—
They skirt the surges, keeping just out of reach
Of the advancing and receding foam.
It is early evening; we have come
To the broad shelf of Amagansett beach,
Haunt of my youth, my spirit's home.

In the enormous dome
Seaward, the horizon is garlanded
With tender clouds; the hollow shell
Of heaven is luminous; the exhausted, pale
Waters exhale
A vast oceanic odor, a sea-soft breath.
Sundown. A sense of absence and of vacancy.
While there is still daylight,
A faint moon-path appears upon the sea;
While yet the living light prevails
Against the encroaching night,
The tenuous light of memory
Sets its cold seal upon
All that is gone—
On the now vanished day,
On the now vanished past.

TELOS

Give me your hand
By these grey waters—
The day is ending.

Already the first
Faint star pierces
The veil of heaven.

Oh, the long way
We two have come,
In joy, together,

To these grey shores
And quiet waters
And the day's ending!

The day is ending.
The journey is ended.
Give me your hand.

DEAR MEN AND WOMEN
(*In Memory of Van Wyck Brooks*)

In the quiet before cockcrow when the cricket's
Mandolin falters, when the light of the past
Falling from the high stars yet haunts the earth
And the east quickens, I think of those I love—
Dear men and women no longer with us.

And not in grief or regret merely but rather
With a love that is almost joy I think of them,
Of whom I am part, as they of me, and through whom
I am made more wholly one with the pain and the glory,
The heartbreak at the heart of things.

I have learned it from them at last, who am now grown old
A happy man, that the nature of things is tragic
And meaningful beyond words, that to have lived
Even if once only, once and no more,
Will have been—oh, how truly—worth it.

The years go by: March flows into April,
The sycamore's delicate tracery puts on
Its tender green; April is August soon;
Autumn, and the raving of insect choirs,
The thud of apples in moonlit orchards;

Till winter brings the slant, windy light again
On shining Manhattan, her towering stone and glass;
And age deepens—oh, much is taken, but one
Dearer than all remains, and life is sweet
Still, to the now enlightened spirit.

Doors are opened that never before were opened,
New ways stand open, but quietly one door
Closes, the door to the future; there it is written,
"Thus far and no farther"—there, as at Eden's gate,
The angel with the fiery sword.

The Eden we dream of, the Eden that lies before us,
The unattainable dream, soon lies behind.
Eden is always yesterday or tomorrow,
There is no way now but back, back to the past—
The past has become paradise.

And there they dwell, those ineffable presences,
Safe beyond time, rescued from death and change.
Though all be taken, they only shall not be taken—
Immortal, unaging, unaltered, faithful yet
To that lost dream world they inhabit.

Truly, to me they now may come no more,
But I to them in reverie and remembrance
Still may return, in me they still live on;
In me they shall have their being, till we together
Darken in the great memory.

Dear eyes of delight, dear youthful tresses, foreheads
Furrowed with age, dear hands of love and care—
Lying awake at dawn, I remember them,
With a love that is almost joy I remember them:
Lost, and all mine, all mine, forever.

FAREWELL TO THE HOUSE
IN BONAC

Above the roof a sunset-colored cloud is shining;
The long light is slant in woodland and in grove;
Light, on lawn and quiet garden;
And everywhere, half-heard, the murmuring of the sea.
So shall I remember you always,
Country of my far childhood,
Refuge throughout all time till now.
Farewell, dear place, dear house.
Farewell, dear people who lived here and who are no more.
Farewell, youth and the dream—
All those years,
Such memories, such memories!
Farewell, farewell,
Cradle and grave of my poems.

HELIOS

Father, in a benign hour,
In the bare solitude of the beaches,
By the naked solitude of the sea,
In the immense solitude of heaven,
You uncovered your face,
And I worshipped you.

In the strict simplicity of light,
To the sound of the sea's thunder,
In the silence of your light,
My music fell from me
Like a forgotten tune.

O all-beholding father,
You who have looked upon the Pharaohs,
And upon the Crucifixion on Golgotha
And the passing generations of mankind,
There came no cloud between us,
Creator and creature were one,
In the bare solitude of the beaches,
By the naked solitude of the sea,
In a benign hour,
In the silence of your light.